Codfather 2

Other books by Jeff Hagen

Betsy

Hiawatha Passing

Steeple Chase

Northern Retreats

Fry Me to the Moon

Codfather 2

AN ILLUSTRATED JOURNEY TO MIDWEST FISH FRIES AND BEYOND

Text and drawings by
Jeff Hagen

Prairie Oak Press
Madison, Wisconsin

First edition, first printing

Copyright © 2001 by Jeff Hagen

All rights reserved. No part of this publication may be reproduced or transmitted in any form or by any means, electronic or mechanical, including photocopy, recording, or any information storage or retrieval system, without permission in writing from the publisher.

Prairie Oak Press
A subsidiary of
Trails Media Group, Inc.
P.O. Box 317
Black Earth, Wisconsin 53515-0317
(800) 236-8088
E-mail: info@wistrails.com
www.trailsbooks.com

Typeset by Quick Quality Press, Madison, Wisconsin

Cover design by Flying Fish Graphics, Blue Mounds, Wisconsin

Printed in Korea

Library of Congress Cataloging-in-Publication Data:

Hagan, Jeff, 1950-
  Codfather 2: an illustrated journey to Midwest fish fries and beyond / text and drawings by Jeff Hagen.--1st ed.
      p. cm.
  Continues: Fry me to the moon.
  ISBN 1-879483-79-3
  1. Restaurants--Middle West--Guidebooks. 2. Bars (Drinking establishments)--Middle West--Guidebooks. 3. Cookery (Fish) 4. Frying. I. Title.

TX907.3.M55 H34 2001
647.9577--dc21   2001032116

To my son Kit

De Ja Moo . . . It's Codfather Two

Contents

Introduction: Blueless in Wisconsin xi

What to Drive to a Fish Fry 1

Vocabulary: What to Say at a Fish Fry 2

Easy Creek (Easy Does It) 4

A Relish Tray of Supper Clubs 8

Trailways Inn 13

Tomorrow River Supper Club . . . Drawn to Water 16

Kropps Supper Club . . . Trees, Planks, and Booyah 18

The Idlewile Inn . . . Holy Grail of the Bloody Mary 20

Two 0 Nine Main . . . Big Fish in a Small Pond 22

Kendall's Smokehouse . . . A Man and a Very Special Dog 24

Emily's Deli . . . Coming Home 26

Trail Center. . . Somewhere on the Gunflint Trail 28

A Tail of Two Cities . . . Tavern on Grand & Gluek's 30

Top Ten Juke Box Hits at a Friday Night Fish Fry 34

Cayuga Hotel Saloon . . . The Best Place in Town to Get Fish 36

Hubbard Avenue Diner . . . A Streamliner in Suburbia 38

Top Ten Rejected License Plate Slogans for Wisconsin 40

The Post House . . . The Very Best for Miles Around 42

Herbster Town Smelt Fry . . . Scoop Dreams 44

Breitbachs Bar & Restaurant . . . Jesse James' First Mistake 46

The Port Hotel . . . "Too Fry For" 48

Gruenke's Restaurant & Inn . . . A Liver Runs Through It 50

Brewery Creek of Mineral Point 52

Partridge Hall . . . The Markings of Time 54

Fitzgerald's Genoa Junction . . . Diner at Eight 56

Lelle's Bar . . . Small Wonder 58

Fireman's Tavern . . . Gone Fishin' 60

The Longbranch Saloon . . . Salt of the Earth 62

Big Top Chautauqua . . . Lake Superior Software 65

Miss Katie's Diner & the Crocus . . . 2 Fry 4 68

The Brett Vette 71

The Platter Restaurant . . . A Platter Full of Goodness 72

Minnesota State Fair . . . They've Got the Whole World on a Stick 74

What the Heck? Tavern . . . Rustic Charm on a Corner in Time 76

Eat My Fish . . . At the End of a Rainbow 78

Bungalow #4 . . . Thoughts from a Small Cabin in the Far North 80

Where to Find Fish 83

A Fisherman's Map of God's Country 84

About the Author 88

Fin 89

A very special thank you to Jerry Minnich,
Dave and Connie Shoemaker,
Jeff Macht, Lee and Rose Englund, Kent Fletcher,
Cindy Stover, Mariel Wozniak,
Bonnie Berens, Debbie Durand, and Princess Rapolano.

Introduction

In my book **Fry Me to the Moon**, I alluded to the reasons behind the popularity of Friday night fish fries in Wisconsin.

One of the major reasons was the fact that Wisconsin did not have the restrictive "blue laws" that encumbered many other states. In a nutshell, these are laws that barred minors from entering restaurants where liquor was served.

These laws vary from state to state in severity and kinds of restrictions. (In recent years, some states have relaxed their laws and enforcement of laws.)

WISCONSIN has a state characteristic that some historians refer to as the German Imbibement Factor, a social habit brought over from the old country in which the whole family goes into an inn, tavern, or eating establishment to EAT, DRINK, AND BE MERRY.

For years, many scholars and travelers have referred to this state's imbibement trait as being BLUELESS IN WISCONSIN.

Indeed, this is a big factor in the fish fry reputation of the Dairy State. But several readers of **Fry Me to the Moon** implored me to give the other states in the Midwest a chance to show off their own hot spots and favorite Friday night haunts that feature excellent fish and wonderful dining adventures.

So, to be fair, I journeyed outward from this fish-fanatic land of Wisconsin and actually CROSSED STATE LINES to visit establishments in our surrounding states of Iowa, Minnesota, Michigan, and Illinois. Let's just call them one territory—a vast land that lies just beyond the driftless land, a place called FINLANDIA.

Follow me. I'll take you there. And show you a sampling of the best I found for miles around.

What to Drive to a Fish Fry

The ideal family fish fry vehicle must be large enough to hold eight kids and one set of parents along with assorted in-laws, grandparents, and the neighborhood boy, Eddie.

The vehicle must be jumbo in scale, made of fortified steel with rust accents. The bumper chrome should not be visible, but, rather, covered with bumper stickers with off-color jokes expressing common state themes of football, fishing, hunting, D.N.R. or "wife" jokes—all in bad taste and all politically incorrect.

The family sedan must be large enough to take up one and a half parking spaces. A working muffler is optional.

Vocabulary

WHAT TO SAY AT A FISH FRY
(SPRECKENZEEEE OSHKOSH?)

Permissible Words and Phrases—An Aid for Out-of-Staters

1. LITTLE G. The small-case "g" does not exist in Wisconsin language. Scholars disagree as to when it became extinct, some claiming it never was there in the formative years of statehood. Instead, the sound of "un" is used in its absence. Used thusly: huntun, fishun, boatun, eatun, and chuggun are commonly heard in table conversation across Dairyland.

   For example, used in conversation, the dialect would sound like this: "Ernie was TOWUN his ice FISHUN shack and CUTTUN cross da lake when he hears a loud CRACKUN sound." In any language, this spells disaster.

2. DARE. In Wisconsin, this means "There," as in "Don't go dare," or in geographical reference, "Dare it is, RIGHT DARE ON DA MAP!"

3. ANSO. In Wisconsin this means "And so." It signifies the impending conclusion of a table conversation. For example, "ANSO finally we got da skunk to come outta da trailer house by bangun on da back wit a sledge hammer and a shovel."

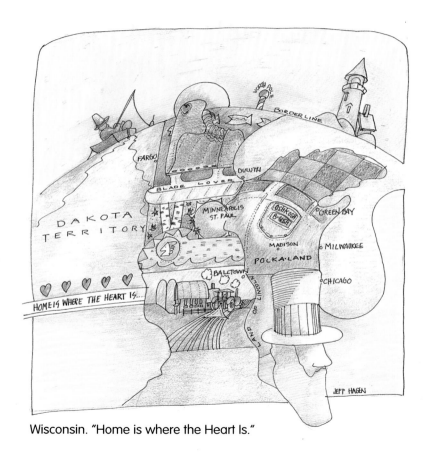

Wisconsin. "Home is where the Heart Is."

Easy Creek (Easy Does It)

The road twists, turns, and undulates along the hills and valleys of Pepin County like a spool of smooth, black satin ribbon unrolling across God's Country.

I'm on a mission.

Several people have told me that there is a tremendous fish fry out here, in a small town tucked away in a deep valley.

The locals call this part of Wisconsin "Coulee Country," so named by early French explorers because of the many fast-moving streams and tributaries running down into the great Mississippi River Valley below.

It is beautiful country. Emerald-green hills capped by faded red barns and bone-white farm houses. Soft blue smoke drifts upward into a cloudless sky, bringing with it the sweet aroma and incense of burning fall leaves.

The town I am looking for is called Arkansaw.

Why Arkansaw? I wonder.

At the crest of a hill, I encounter a small town sign which reads: ARKANSAW. POPULATION 210. UNINCORPORATED.

As I stop to look at the sign, I can hear the soft putt-putt sound of a tractor coming over the hill. A vintage Allis-Chalmers pulls up to me at the sign. I wave and motion the driver to come over to my car. I have a question for him.

With a loud backfire report, he shuts down the tractor and ambles over to me.

It has been my experience in finding these fish fries that the best guide is usually a local who looks as if he has been "in these parts" for some time. This guy fits the bill. He leans on the sign, toothpick in mouth, and says, "What kin I do fer ya?"

"Well, I heard that there is a great fish fry in town. Where is it?"

"Which one?" he replies.

"WHICH ONE!!! 210 people and you have more than one?"

"Oh, yeah, of course."

And I realize, of course, that this is Wisconsin and we DO HAVE OUR PRIORITIES.

EASY DOES IT

Easy Creek Bistro and Bar

Well, I found the fish fry that I was looking for in this tiny town. The one I had heard about was Easy Creek Bistro and Bar. It's smack-dab in the middle of town. A great place with big-city culinary offerings and a great creekside location.

I wondered why a small town in Wisconsin was named after another state. Well, the story goes that, in 1852, an early settler named Willard F. Holbrook took a day off from work at a nearby sawmill to GO FISHING (sounds like something we might do today). They came to this spot and named it Arkansaw because it reminded them of the state of Arkansas. They used a "w" at the end to give the place some unique distinction.

Holbrook continued to come back to fish for trout. Eventually he built a log cabin and started a furniture factory.

Arkansaw is a town with a strong piscatorial heritage. There is a legend here that, before Holbrook came wandering through the woods, the Indians would not fish here for trout. They believed that the bountiful brook trout kept the waters pure and sacred.

Easy Creek Bistro

A Relish Tray of Supper Clubs

OK, so what's the deal with all these supper clubs in Wisconsin, and why do they ALL HAVE THE SAME RELISH TRAYS AND MENU OFFERINGS?

You walk into a supper club in Hurley. A waitress, in a starched black-and-red uniform with the name "Gert" on her blouse pocket, greets you and places a big chrome revolving relish carousel in the center of your table.

You peer over the lip of the various compartments in the carousel and notice a familiar pallet of pickled beets, three-bean salad, cheese spread, crinkled carrots, scallions, radish florets, and celery stalks. A little wicker basket of breadsticks and crackers rides along as a sidekick. You think, "Hey, I've seen this before." In fact, EVERY SUPPER CLUB IN THE STATE has this same culinary curriculum.

Let's see, what kind of pre-supper drink shall I have? I see, I have four choices: brandy, a brandy Manhattan, a brandy old-fashioned, and a brandy Alexander. Hmmm, I think I'll have a brandy Alexander. Good choice! Bonnie, my dining companion, is impressed with my worldliness. I have, after all, traveled fear-lessly across the state line on several previous occasions. Or is she laughing at my tie that I've just dragged across the cottage cheese compartment?

But hey, what about these supper clubs? I mean, why and when did they take root here and flourish, thus becoming an important part of Wisconsin culture?

I talked with several owners and bartenders, and this is what I heard:

Onalaska
Bluegill

The supper club seems to have started in Wisconsin back in the 1930s and '40s. The story goes that many communities had a limited allocation of liquor licenses, and many of those were already taken. So, the supper club was an alternative, operating under a new category that allowed a limited liquor license. Under the agreement, the club would begin serving only at supper time (after 5 p.m.) and would serve liquor until closing.

One of my sources told me that the "sneeze shield" over the salad bar was invented at a supper club in northern Wisconsin! Hey, California may have given us the computer microchip—BUT MANKIND OWES THANKS TO WISCONSIN FOR THE SNEEZE SHIELD!

Another common denominator of the supper club in Wisconsin is the menu. It's a calendar thing. Look at your watch to see which day of the week it is. If it's Friday, IT'S FISH FRY NIGHT. If it's Saturday night, IT'S PRIME RIB NIGHT. And if it's Sunday afternoon, it's got to be BAKED CHICKEN. Many of these establishments named their supper clubs after the highway that passed by their front doors. For instance, Club 26 fronts Highway 26, near Milton and Fort Atkinson.

The reality of this became apparent to me when I was attempting to interview a supper club owner and called long distance information to find her number. I wasn't sure which town the club was nearest, so I asked the operator to give me the listing for suppper clubs that were followed by a number. HOLY SMOKE! CLUB 26. CLUB 13. CLUB 51. CLUB 18. The list went on and on. I got the picture.

No matter what the number, though, they all have a common denominator, going much deeper than the relish tray. They offer visitors a carousal filled with friendliness, good service, good food, laughter, and fun, all found in great abundance tucked away in the Northland. Here is a sampling of several that I found.

Club 26

Sky Lawn

Trailways Inn

When I first moved to Wisconsin, several good friends implored me to go with them to a "fish fry."

"OK, I'm game, let's go." So we made eight o'clock reservations and set out for the big night. When we arrived at the supper club, we found a parking lot packed with cars. Upon entering the lobby, we informed the waitress that we had reservations at eight. "Good," she replied. "Have a seat in the bar and we'll call you."

The bar was crowded and noisy, but friendly and congenial in atmosphere. An hour passed. I realized that reservations didn't seem to count for much. In fact, EVERYONE HERE HAS A RESERVATION FOR EIGHT O'CLOCK!

So I decided to sit back and relax and get into the atmosphere of Friday night in Wisconsin. Then, somewhere during the second hour, a voice came out of the darkness. "Hagen, party of six."

The hostess led us through the crowd like a well-seasoned pathfinder. A pilot fish in a sea of humanity. We snaked and dipped through several busy rooms, down a level, up into the mezzanine, and there was our table, by a window overlooking a snowy backyard of birch trees, bird feeders, and swaying jack pines.

Trailways Inn

We sat down. I looked around. We were surrounded by amber-colored knotty pine, stuffed animal heads, and black-and-white photos of beaming fishermen holding up trophy-size muskies. The atmosphere fit.

The fish dinner turned out to be worth the wait, and I went away feeling well-nourished both in a culinary and a cultural sense.

A great place in the Northwoods to experience both is the Trailways Inn, near Hayward. The atmosphere here is cozy and casual. At the end of the bar is a Franklin fireplace, crackling and purring away. People are chatting and laughing, in no apparent hurry, enjoying each other's company.

Something about this picture speaks of home. A sense of place, a sense of community, and a sense of belonging, all tucked together in a pine-scented dining room deeply rooted in the heart and soul of Wisconsin.

Drawn to Water

Tomorrow River Supper Club

When I was growing up in Minnesota, we lived on a bluff overlooking a river and its broad emerald-green valley that stretched for miles far off into the horizon.

Our parents warned us, "Don't go down near that river!" And, of course, they were right to worry. For, with seasonal regularity, the river took its toll of unfortunate souls who disappeared and drowned beneath its chocolate-brown surface. Being kids, however, we went anyway.

We were drawn to the river as if it were some kind of magical place filled with danger and adventure, pulling us along with its rippling current.

I grew up with that fascination. Still have it. Something to do with my soul and spirit of adventure. But it also has something to do with relaxing and slowing down the speed of life.

So it should come as no surprise that, when we arrived at this riverside supper club and sat down at a window overlooking the Tomorrow River to enjoy a fish dinner, I was entranced.

This is a "soft" river—shallow, slow, and lazy. Yet the allure is obvious. As I sat gazing at the bronze-tinted water flowing past our window, I felt that time was suspended. No rush. No hurry.

Just a tranquil perspective in which to savor the present moment . . . here . . . on the edge of Tomorrow.

Tomorrow River Supper Club

Trees, planks, and booyah

Kropp's Supper Club

Located on the outskirts of Green Bay is a proud little establishment, one of the oldest and best fish fries in Wisconsin.

In the beginning, more than 150 years ago, this little settlement was called Mill Center. The area was dense with beech, maple, oak, pine, ash, birch, and basswood trees. The town became a major hub in the lumber industry. For twenty years it was labeled "The greatest milling section in Wisconsin." More than thirty mills operated in Mill Center in its heyday.

About this time, the plank road craze hit the area. Plank roads offered a weather-resistant road surface. The construction involved laying down a double timber track which, in turn, was covered with heavy wooden planks. It was incredibly labor-intensive, but very popular in its day. The town evolved from a milling center to a popular stopover for travelers heading for Green Bay.

In 1904, Edward Lawler built the town's tavern, food, and lodging establishment. That building became a local landmark. In 1947, Clarence and Isabelle Kropp purchased the place and opened the supper club that bears their name.

In the early days of Kropp's Supper Club, Isabelle fried fish in cast-iron pans in the basement. Back then, the cost of a fish fry was 35 cents!

Over the years, Kropp's became THE place to go for fish, and the place on Sunday afternoons where one could watch the Packers on TV and indulge in brandy and booyah, a chicken-and-vegetable soup of Belgian origin.

Today, another generation of Kropp's operates the establishment, maintaining the wonderful service, food, and tradition started nearly a century ago.

Kropp's Supper Club

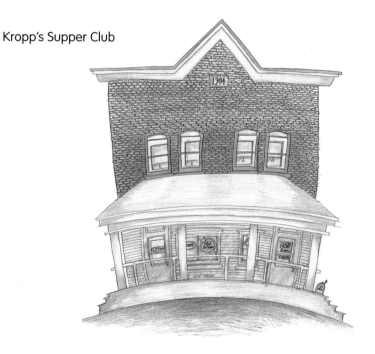

The Idlewile Inn

Not long ago, I had the opportunity to travel to Paris. One of the places I wanted to visit was Harry's New York Bar, an old haunt of Hemingway, Fitzgerald, and other literary luminaries of a bygone era.

Prior to the trip, I read about Harry's and learned that it was the birthplace of the Bloody Mary. According to the bartender's story, it was Hemingway who helped inspire the drink.

Well, I reasoned, I am in Paris, this is Harry's. What else to order than a Bloody Mary? I mean, it's PART OF THE HISTORY OF CIVILIZED MAN.

I wish I could report that it was a great experience—you know, one of those moments when the world stops for a moment of extreme ecstasy. Naaah, it was disappointing to say the least.

That moment of ecstasy did come to me. But not at Harry's. Not in France. It arrived in a place thousands of miles and a world apart from that dark street in Paris.

It occurred when I sat down to eat at a charming little bistro in the small town of St. Cloud, Wisconsin, at the Idlewile Inn.

The waitress asked me whether I would like a drink before dinner. I ordered a Bloody Mary. And THIS ONE was a work of art. Smooth and

Harry's of Paris

delicious, garnished with a stalk of asparagus, sipped in slow and deliberate pleasure.

At that moment, I realized the irony of the experience. Yes, the inception of this popular drink may have been in Paris, but the PERFECTION of same can be found at a window seat in a small eatery, deep in the heart of Mid-America.

The Idlewile Inn

Big Fish in a Small Pond

Two O Nine Main

Over the years, I have had the privilege to dine in a variety of restaurants in big cities, both in the U.S. and abroad. Many of them provided fine food and an enjoyable experience.

But none of them even came close to the quality of food and service that we encountered at this tiny eatery in rural Wisconsin.

The tiny burg of Monticello is located deep in the heart of cheese country, near the Swiss-American village of New Glarus. On the night that we arrived there, the town was holding its annual outdoor celebration. As we walked up to the front of this vintage building, the fireworks show began, sending huge pink and emerald rockets up into the ebony sky directly behind the restaurant. I took this as a positive omen, and I wasn't disappointed with the dining experience that followed.

Two O Nine Main is owned and operated by a young couple who worked in a number of elegant restaurants in Madison. A few years back they decided to leave the city and seek more bucolic environs out in rural Dairyland.

Fortunately for diners, they bought this little Main Street building and opened a restaurant to display their considerable talents.

Our table had delicious spring rolls made with smoked trout and ginger, and a variety of delicious menu offerings. But the hit of the evening clearly was the swordfish.

Frankly, I've always believed that ocean fish tastes best at restaurants NEAR THE OCEAN. But this place, and the talent of its chef, changed my mind. The crowning moment of that epiphany came at dessert time, as I sat back savoring the crème brulée while looking out at the exploding sky rockets . . . and thinking . . . Somehow all this fits—the place, the food, the people, the realization that in the smallest of places lie the greatest of rewards.

Two O Nine Main

Kendall's Smokehouse

It was snowing on the day that I pulled in here. Snowflakes the size of silver dollars floated down out of a steel-grey sky. I parked my car in front of this roadside building and looked around. Not much was happening, other than an occasional car whining by and the soft rhythm of falling snow.

I stepped into the building and found an interior well-stocked with fish, cheese, crackers, and beer. But nobody was behind the counter, save a big, friendly, tail-wagging dog. It took one look at me and turned around and exited the room via a swinging door.

A few minutes later, a kindly looking gent, who reminded me of my Norwegian uncle, Ibsen, came strolling out through the same door. His name was Russ Kendall.

"Charlie came and got me. He's a good dog. He's a good friend."

So it began that I started a habit of stopping to see this man and his dog. I would usually pick up whitefish or lake trout that Russ had caught out on the big lake. We always had a warm conversation. Usually, the fish came wrapped in a story about his wonderful dog and companion, Charlie.

Later, when I pulled off the road to eat the fish, I found I could enjoy two meals from Russ. One satisfied my pallet, savoring maple-cured, smoked fish; the other satisfying my soul, a story about that smart dog, Charlie.

Both left me grinning and well nourished for the journey ahead.

Russ Kendall's Smokehouse

Emily's Deli

On the other edge of town rests a vintage building that serves as a post office, general store, inn, deli, and a great place to experience a fish boil.

For the record, a fish boil harks back to a day when each one of these little fishing villages on the Great Lakes hummed with activity. As the armada of fishing boats returned to their shoreline villages, a great celebration was held, and a major part of it was the fish boil, a cooking process in which fish were tossed into boiling caldrons of water along with potatoes to roll in a furious boil. The process was accentuated by flames that ignited the fish oil on the surface of the boiling pot.

As the fish boiled, people played guitars and fiddles, and ate, drank, and danced in communal gratification for the safe return of seafaring souls.

Now the fleets are history. Their memories appear as graying driftwood, tumbling upon the sands of time.

Today, Emily's preserves a small corner of that beloved tradition, somewhat modified in that the fish is boiled in the kitchen and not out on the shore. But it has the feel and taste of a little community of neighbors and friends who gather together in communal celebration. A time spent together to praise the tradition of those souls from long ago, those who devoted their lives to coming home with an abundant harvest and high spirits.

Emily's Deli

TRUE NORTH

Trail Center

Just a short jog down the trail from Hungry Jack Road rests a little outpost of humanity where a weary traveler can indulge in a delicious meal, surrounded by an atmosphere of Northwoods rustic charm.

The interior of this little tin-roofed log building is covered with stuffed moose heads, snowshoes, beaver pelts, vintage road signs, antiques, artifacts, and photographs of beaming sunburned fishermen hefting huge trophy fish out of sky-blue waters. For this is True North, and Trail Center is a great place to spend a night dining on fish and other delicious menu offerings.

What is not on the menu, but still available in abundant supply, is the healthful, good humored attitude of the owner and staff. It is apparent that these people know how to have a good time! Even on the coldest of northern Minnesota nights, these people serve up humor by the platter full.

On any given night, the people who work here are prone to start the crowd singing and dancing. When Cajun music pops from the juke box, the bartender straps on one of those wearable Cajun washboards and commences to lead the crowd in song.

And up here, in the deep Northwoods, just a stone's throw away from the Canadian border, all of this fits. Good food and good times, in a warm and cozy setting. It's a combination that I believe even the old French voyageurs would have enjoyed, and would have exclaimed, "LAISEZ LES BON TEMPS ROULER!" Indeed, let the good times roll.

Trail Center

A Tail of Two Cities

The Tavern on Grand, St. Paul

Gluek's, Minneapolis

They are the best of friends.

They are the worst of enemies.

One is Neo-Scandinavian Lutheran.

The other is Old World European Catholic.

For decades they have fought "Sports Wars" over which would land the next professional franchise team. And WHERE WOULD THE STADIUM OR ARENA BE LOCATED.

The rest of the world would know them as "TWINS."

Twins? Hardly. I grew up in the Twin Cities. As I remember, it was always an issue of "two different worlds, two different opinions."

Sometimes they were friends. Sometimes they were arch enemies. Sometimes they were tolerable kin. But, one thing they have always shared in common is a love for good food. Both cities have excellent dining spots.

Naturally, in a state that is noted for its 10,000 lakes and an abundance of fresh-water fish, a restaurant with fish on the menu is bound to draw attention.

Here are two fine representatives of the Twin Cities piscatorial scene:

The Tavern on Grand has a great Walleye Shore lunch. And

Gluek's, in downtown Minneapolis, offers a tasty little fish fry on Friday nights.

The Tavern on Grand

Glueck's

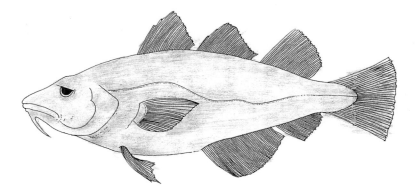

Thank Cod . . . It's Friday!

Top Ten Jukebox Hits
at a Friday Night Fish Fry

10. I Believe I Can Fry!

9. I'm In with the Fin Crowd . . . Petula Carp

8. Fa . . . Lay . . . La . . . Eric Plankton

7. Once, Twice, Three Times a Crappie

6. Selected hits from the Catholic Wedding Polka Medley Album
    (Note: Extra coins required.)

5. Tuna, Luna, Lura . . . (Just an Irish Lullaby)

4. Smeltin' Safari

3. Big Girls Don't Fry (That's Just an Alibi)

2. Dat ain't No Ordinary Eel . . . Dat's a Moray!!!

1. It's My Party . . . and I'll Fry If I Want To

THE BEST PLACE IN TOWN TO GET FISH

Cayuga Hotel Saloon

Now this is the definitive Up North fish fry. The best place in town to get fish.

How can I make that claim, you ask?

Because it's the ONLY place in town to get fish.

Also, it happens to be the ONLY BUILDING IN TOWN—PERIOD. In other words, IT IS THE TOWN . . . THE WHOLE TOWN.

Even though it has no competition, and doesn't need to prove anything, I found that it ranked up there in the top five places that I traveled to for fish. Their walleye dinner is superb!

It's Cayuga. And I asked the bartender how the town got its name. Was it named after a local Indian chief?

"Nope," she replied, "it came from New York."

It seems that, many years ago, Cornell University purchased large tracts of land up here to study the geology of the area. Since they owned the surrounding land, they needed a name for the train station and settlement.

So they named it after Lake Cayuga, in Ithaca, New York, the home of Cornell University.

Cayuga Hotel Saloon

Hubbard Avenue Diner

I grew up in the 1950s during a time when cross-country travel consisted of two-lane blacktop highways. Much of the roadside archaeology of that era consisted of Burma Shave signs, Map-and-Pa groceries, Flying Red Horse filling stations, and roadside diners.

I loved them all and was saddened over the years to see them slowly fade from the American roadside. I've always had an affinity for roadside diners. Maybe it was the ruby-red neon beaming late into the night. To me, growing up in the Midwest, they were like nocturnal totems spread across the prairie.

Many diners were built by the Valentine Manufacturing Company (in Wichita, Kansas) from prefabricated kits. They were shipped across the country to tiny urban and rural lots, where they were reassembled and opened for business.

Some of the old ones still exist. (The Dixie Diner, near Lafayette, Indiana, and Mickey's Diner in downtown St. Paul). But most have gone the way of the buffalo, done in by the Interstate Highway System and fast-food drive-through franchise chains.

Fortunately, I found a new eating spot that combines the charm of those old-timers with a harmonious menu of contemporary dishes, including a FRIDAY NIGHT FISH FRY.

This place has great food! Comfortably appointed with spacious interior glass, chrome, overstuffed booths, and soft cream-colored lighting. Humming above the clatter and chatter of patrons are the melodies of blues, jazz, and the big band sound of another era.

Hubbard Avenue Diner

Top Ten Rejected License Plate Tourist Slogans for the State of Wisconsin

10. Wisconsin: Fry It and They Will Come

9. Wisconsin: In Heaven There is No Beer,
   That's Why We Drink It Here

8. Wisconsin: Milk It for All It's Worth

7. Wisconsin: Come Fry With Me

6. Wisconsin: The Prime Rib State

5. Wisconsin: Highest Cholesterol Level on Planet Earth

4. Wisconsin: The Nation's Leader in Brats, Beer, and Cow Methane

3. Wisconsin: Fit to be Fried

2. Wisconsin: To Err is Human, to Moo is Bovine

1. Wisconsin: We Don't Care if ESPN Teases, We'll Keep Wear-Un Our Plastic Hats of Cheezahs!!!

DRIVING MISS DAISY

The Post House

Late one afternoon, I stopped at a small grocery store to buy provisions and to scout out a good fish fry in the town.

Midway between the soap isle and the canned corn display, I struck up a conversation with three local shoppers and asked the question, "Where is the best place in town to go for fish?"

Their collective answer surprised me. "There isn't a good one here, but there's a great one over in Spring Green!"

I hastened to reply, "But that's thirty miles away!"

"So what! Hey, this is Wisconsin! A thirty-mile drive is nothin'."

It was this enthusiastic endorsement from miles away that drew me to the place they all mentioned, the Post House in Frank Lloyd Wright's beloved home of Spring Green.

We had a great fish dinner here in the oldest continuously operated eatery in Wisconsin.

After the fish fry was over, I related the story about the grocery store conversation to the hostess and she didn't seem fazed about the glowing recommendations from afar. In fact, she said, they have regulars who come every Friday night, from more than fifty miles away—"even on nights when we have storms or heavy snows."

The Post House

SCOOP DREAMS

Herbster Town Smelt Fry

If you followed the journey in **Fry Me to the Moon**, you already know that catching smelt is a "skill-optional" activity involving beer and common house-hold fishing gear—usually, a plastic bucket, a discarded net, or a plastic shopping bag from Target or K-Mart.

Whatever the choice, the smelt fisherman fearlessly wades into the bone-chilling water of late winter to scoop smelt from the raging stream.

In recent years, folks along Lake Superior have noticed a decline in the number of smelt running up the rivers. The explanations have ranged from the idea that larger fish are eating the smelt, to environmental pollution and tampering of the lakes' fish populations. Regardless of the reasons, there is one place you can count on, for finding smelt: In the tiny fishing village of Herbster, Wisconsin, located on the south shore of Lake Superior.

But these smelt wouldn't be running. They come to you cooked and ready for your culinary pleasure.

Every spring for the past 25 years, the Herbster Community Club has held their annual smelt fry on the third Saturday in April. The setting of the event is unique. It takes place in the oldest (and perhaps only) log gym in the state of Wisconsin. In the 1940s the WPA built this gym out of local pine and native stone.

For years, gangly high school kids pounded the hardwoods, running up and down the floor, accompanied by rhythmic cheers and screaming crowds. That ended in the 1970s, however, when the little town schools around here consolidated into one big high school located down the highway from Herbster. But all is not forgotten, for there is that one day in April when the sweet memories of fading jump shots converge with the delicious aroma of frying fish.

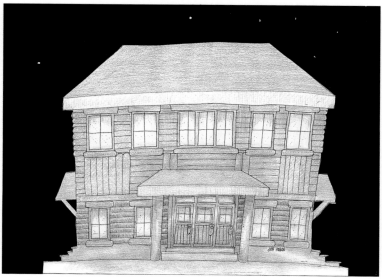

Herbster Log Gym

Breitbach's Bar & Restaurant

They say this is the oldest bar in the state of Iowa. It dates way back to 1852.

In its early days, more than a century ago, two mysterious horsemen came riding in and checked into one of the upstairs rooms. The midnight duo rode ponies that showed a heavy coat of sweat, like they had been riding hard for a long spell.

Odd, that the riders slept only a few hours before riding off just before dawn. But one of them accidentally left a horse blanket in the stable. Not a remarkable blanket, except for the name embroidered on its side: **Frank James**. He and his famous brother Jesse had picked this roadhouse to rest for the night on their way north to an infamous bank robbery in Northfield, Minnesota

Over the years, scores of people, both the famous and the unknown, have walked through these doors to pause on their journeys. Nowadays, it no longer accommodates overnight guests, but it has established its own legend— a reputation for great food and warm hospitality that even the James gang would have appreciated, had they changed their plans and stayed longer.

Dining tip: The fish fry is great, but don't pass up the raspberry pie! It's tasty enough to rob a bank for.

Balltown

"To Fry For"

The Port Hotel

The story goes that back in the late 1950s or early '60s, a tanned, attractive gentleman arrived in town, accompanied by a group of friends.

He was in dire need of a haircut. So he stopped at the Port Hotel and descended the steps to the hotel barbershop where he was obliged with a quick trim.

Nothing unusual about this, until some of the locals noticed that he looked familiar and that the "friends" clustered around him were neither kin nor cohorts, but iron-packing Secret Service agents.

The man with the new haircut? Jack Kennedy. He was traveling through Port Washington while campaigning for the presidency of the United States.

Well, J.F.K. and the barbershop have passed into history, along with a thousand other stories in this century-old hotel. But it's still here for you to enjoy.

That joy may easily be found on a Friday night when you can sit down in the dining room and indulge in a delicious meal of fresh walleye. Savor that first bite. . . ummmmm . . . it's history in the making.

The Port Hotel

A LIVER RUNS THROUGH IT

Greunke's Restaurant & Inn

This place has it all. Legend, location, and the lure of fresh Lake Superior white-fish cooking in an iron kettle on Main Street.

The aroma of smoked fish is second nature here. For this town has a deep tradition of fishermen who ventured with their small wooden crafts out onto the great silver lake to seek bountiful harvests.

Whitefish from the lake is boiled in an open kettle along with sweet baby red potatoes and succulent onions. Add to this delicious trio fresh-cut coleslaw, dark, aromatic bread, and delicious pie made with fruit picked from the local hills.

Now, picture eating this truly Northern chow in a charming and cozy century-old inn filled with laughing people. The inn is complete with knotty-pine woodwork and a Wurlitzer jukebox stacked with original 78 RPM records from the 1930s. The place even has an old-fashioned soda fountain complete with a soda jerk.

If you're so inclined to "eat like the natives," here's your challenge: Try ordering whitefish livers. This place is famous for them. They are dipped in batter, lightly fried, and served on a bed of lettuce with lemon wedges, homemade tarter sauce, and golden toast points. Try that, and you'll be part of the local "Inn crowd."

Up here, some people call that . . . "In with the FIN crowd."

Greunke's Restaurant & Inn

Brewery Creek Of Mineral Point

A common belief of people who visit Wisconsin is that the fine art of brewing beer began in Milwaukee, by who else? Germans, right?

Wrong. It all began in the mining settlement of Mineral Point in 1835, when a Cornish immigrant by the name of John Phillips started a small brewery. This was five years before the first Milwaukee brewery came into existence.

Come to think of it, Mineral Point was the place where the phrase "Wisconsin Badgers" was coined. It refers to some of the miners who burrowed into hillside caves to sleep, and who were then called "badgers."

Well, of course, both beer and badgers went on to become legendary icons of our state.

Carrying on that tradition, in modern fashion, is a new brewery built in an old warehouse located on the edge of this historic town. The Brewery Creek Inn and Pub is an eatery, a microbrewery, and a guest lodge—a perfect place to toast the night away in the Land of Badgers and Brewmeisters.

The Brewery Creek Brewing Company

The Markings of Time

Partridge Hall

I have this curiosity about how little country towns acquired their names.

When I first looked at a map of Wisconsin, years ago, I noticed the tiny burg of Argyle. I imagined a flock of wool sweater-clad Scottish settlers arriving here in the early 1800s. The Scots must have come to a high overlook, peered down on a countryside of rolling hills covered with interlocking diamond-shaped patterns of prairie grass and proclaimed, "Now, this looks like home!

OK, so the landscape doesn't look like an argyle sock, the cows don't have diamond-shaped markings, and those aren't Scottish tams lying in the pasture. So how did it get its name?

Back in 1844, a group of early settlers applied to Washington for a post office, calling the spot Hazel Green. Well, try again, said the folks in Washington, because THERE ALREADY IS A TOWN CALLED HAZEL GREEN.

Enter one Scottish settler named Allen Wright, who suggested that the town should be named Argyle, in honor of the Duke of Argyle.

In 1878, Argyle received a major addition when an elegant building was constructed by Alanson Partridge. It cost $2,000, which was a big-ticket item in those days. The original north wing served as a carpenter shop where Partridge built furniture. The second floor was used as a performance hall, serving up entertainment for dinners and dances. The building became known as Partridge Hall.

Over the next half-century, Partridge Hall evolved into a grand place for hosting masquerade balls, proms, roller skating, lectures, and basketball games. In 1920 the hall became the Star Theater, showing silent films. Some local history buffs claim that Mary Pickford made an appearance at the Star back in the early days of American cinema.

Like many towns across the land, this one has a favorite son, a local celebrity who grew up here and went on to national prominence. "Fighting Bob" LaFollette spent his boyhood years in Argyle before going on to become a U.S. senator, Wisconsin governor, Progressive Party founder, and eventual presidential candidate.

Today, Partridge Hall is still thriving, with a dining and lodging facility that serves up a great fish fry of a quality and character fitting the patterns of history that made this town an important place in which to linger on the dusty trail of time.

Partridge Hall

DINNER AT EIGHT

Fitzgerald's Genoa Junction

How can you go wrong walking into a charming eight-sided historic building that was built by a man whose first name was WELCOME?

Welcome J. Miller was a carriage and wagon manufacturer back in 1849. Back in those days, an octagonal house was a sure sign of status in our country. More than two thousand of the structures were built in the United States. Most of the octagons were constructed in larger cities such as San Francisco, but a few popped up in rural America, and Welcome was one individual who brought this unique house to Dairyland.

Thirty-six of those eight-sided wonders were constructed in Wisconsin between the years 1844 and 1905. Today, just a few survive. Fortunately, this one in Genoa City is not only surviving—it's thriving.

Over the years it has evolved into a restaurant with an impeccable reputation. People drive from miles around to partake in the fish boil featured at Fitzgerald's, a delicious Friday night feast served year 'round.

A word of advice: Get there early, for the line stretches out the front door and down the walk. But it's worth the wait, for the food is good, the atmosphere is congenial, and the WELCOME mat has been out for over a century and a half.

Fitzgerald's Genoa Junction

SMALL WONDER

Lelle's Bar

As I travel down dusty country roads winding through the driftless land of Wisconsin, I can't help but wonder: What brought these people to these places?

Agriculture, mining, dairying, homestead opportunity, ethnic grouping of immigrant families, good luck and bad luck and the freedom to operate your own farm in God's Country.

To ponder these thoughts also causes me to wonder what happened to cause so many of these little settlements to fade, disappear, or become just bedroom communities without a viable Main Street?

It is sad to drive through these towns and to see a row of boarded-up buildings where there was once was a thriving thoroughfare of mercantile activity. Worse, once-proud buildings of architectural charm and signature are now covered with tacky facades and cheap day-glow signs advertising Video rentals and liquidators' warehouses.

Fortunately, not all these towns have lost their sense of place. One such is Woodford, a tiny village located on the edge of the driftless area. Years ago, it was a railroad and mill town. Today it has just a few surviving buildings. But the town still has heart, in the form of a creekside tavern called LELLE'S.

One of Lelle's features is an outstanding Friday night fish fry.

Just how outstanding, you ask? Well, the village has a population of about 60. The fish fry at Lelle's draws upwards of 300 on Friday nights. Do the math. That's a pretty respectable draw. (If New York City had a fish fry this successful, it would draw 40 million people!)

It's no secret that its attraction is not just happenstance. Rather, it's the result of hard work, and a living spirit of survival, that keeps this little establishment humming. No small achievement these days, to find a SMALL WONDER like Lelle's, alive and well, deep in the heartland of America.

Lelle's Bar

Fireman's Tavern

Much of the credit for the recommendations and research for the fish fry offerings in this book come from you, the invaluable reader.

When **Fry Me to the Moon** was published, I asked (on radio talk shows and in the press) for suggestions for new places to check out.

The response was overwhelming. I am both enlightened and thankful to all those people who took time to send me letter, cards, and e-mails with "hot tips" for favorite fish fries out there in Dairyland and beyond.

One of the more enthusiastic responses came to me from a group of coworkers at a small company in Wisconsin. They started a tradition of a Fish Fry Tour. Each month, one of the group (we'll call them the Cod Squad) would take a turn suggesting a new fish fry to check out. They used **Fry Me to the Moon** as a sort of deep-fried gazetteer.

Here's one of their finds, in their own words:

"Dear Jeff: We found a great place in Columbus, Wisconsin, called the Fireman's Tavern. What we like about it: It has the largest fish selection that we've seen. More than 12 types of fish on the menu, plus 8 different kinds of potatoes, along with many homemade soups and desserts, not to mention over a hundred different beer labels (most in bottles) from standard favorites to local brews. Also, a big plus is that it serves fish not only on Friday but also on Wednesdays and Saturdays. Well worth checking out."

> In Cod We Trust,
> Angie Medenwaldt

Fireman's Tavern

SALT OF THE EARTH

The Longbranch Saloon

Winter had just shed its icy coat when we decided to take a road trip through the LAND OF LINCOLN.

Just south of Chicago, the sun came out, the temperature climbed, and spring in full glory rose to greet us on our journey. HEY, IT WAS THE FIRST DAY OF SPRING! So we decided to take the top down on the convertible and enjoy the countryside.

Speeding along, from the perspective of a breezy roadster, we could enjoy a panorama of open farm country. Miles ahead, I could see a sharp profile reaching upward into the sky from a huge church surrounded by a small settlement and a cluster of maple trees. A long line of parked cars and pickup trucks stretched out of the grove and far down the only road leading to town. What was going on here?

Curiosity and the freedom of the open road got the best of me. So I turned off the highway and traveled down that car-lined road to the little settlement that bore the uncommon name of L'Erable. It was a very small town (population 100) with just two community buildings. One was St. John the Baptist Catholic Church. The other was a little wood-frame tavern that had streams of people passing through its front door.

The Longbranch Saloon

I asked a young couple who walked out of the tavern, "Why are all these people in town? Is there a wedding?"

"Hell, no. It's a FISH FRY at the Longbranch!"

Naturally, we joined the gang and indulged. (Hey, as the old saying goes, "When in Rome . . .")

During the course of a great meal and friendly conversation, we learned some brief history about the town. The little village has its roots in the heritage of French Canadians who settled here in the 1850s. L'Erable is French for Maple Tree. The beautiful church, built in 1873, is the largest frame church standing in Illinois.

Back in 1918, the town started to burn. As the flames engulfed one building after another, someone had the presence of mind to command, "Open the barrels of salt in the store and throw it on the furniture!" Then the people climbed to the rooftops and scattered salt on everything combustible. This stroke of genius saved L'Erable from burning to the ground.

Salt?

Ahh, the things you discover when you turn off the high-speed road of life and linger in a small place that honors the heritage of its church, the pride of its local watering hole, and the ingenuity of its ancestors. It was they who discovered that something as simple as common salt can save a town as uncommon as L'Erable.

LAKE SUPERIOR SOFTWARE

Big Top Chautauqua

Now for something completely different. A tent. A great big tent located in the hills looking out over Lake Superior.

In this great tent, in the summertime, on Friday nights, there is a traditional fish boil. It's a great way to eat fresh fish, but the real attraction here is what comes after dinner. And that's superb entertainment under the big top of a vintage circus tent.

Perhaps you didn't know this, but, a century ago, this kind of event was not uncommon. Chatauquas, like the circus, traveled across this great country, offering variety acts, humor, educational lectures, and popular American music.

That tradition was revived here sixteen years ago. A risky venture at best, but it worked, and now it has become an integral part of the culture in this part of the Northland.

After dinner on any given night, you may experience the joy of watching and listening to such diverse talents and luminaries as Emmy Lou Harris, Leon Redbone, Asleep at the Wheel, Merle Haggard, Mason Williams, Vassar Clements, Claudia Schmidt, Taj Mahal, John Hiatt, Riders in theSky, Don McLean, and many other regional and national singers, musicians, and storytellers. Plus, the Big Top has a talent collection of its own, originally written and staged performances spotlighting local history, legend, and humor.

Big Top Chautauqua

It's a great experience to sit and savor the fish, the music, and the atmosphere of an entertaining evening spent high up in the timber above Lake Superior. Music drifts up, like chimney smoke, spreading out across swaying jack pines before drifting down to the edge of lapping waters.

In between songs, somewhere off in the dark indigo night, a loon trills back as if to bridge the two worlds of man and nature.

Two different worlds. But tonight, they strike a harmonious chord under the stars, the northern lights, and a big blue tent that ripples softly in nocturnal winds.

2 Fry 4

Miss Katie's Diner . . . Crocus

This city has a reputation for an abundant supply of neighborhood taverns, cafes, and unique eateries serving good food along with the frothy suds that "Made Milwaukee Famous."

Two of the best in town are located in two different corners of town.

Miss Katie's Diner is located in the Marquette University neighborhood and gives a new definition to the phrase, "power lunch." Perhaps a better label for this eatery would be "Where the powerful lunch." For this is the little diner that powerful world leaders such as president Bill Clinton and German chancellor Helmut Kohl chose to dine when they visited Milwaukee.

On the south side of town is a quaint little Polish restaurant called Crocus. There are no international luminaries here, just a tremendous menu and a fish fry that offers great potato pancakes on the side.

Besides the fish fry, the Crocus menu offers a great variety of Polish dishes and soups, including Pierogi, White Barscz, and aromatic dill pickle soup.

Two great places in a city that made beer famous. I think it's time for that reputation to include FOOD that made Milwaukee famous.

The Brett Vette

In Wisconsin, it seems that every corner of the state has at least one town where an eccentric Packer fan has painted the silo or propane gas tank to reflect the Green and Gold religion emanating from Green Bay.

Sometimes the religious icon takes the form of a mailbox or a lawn mower.

On one occasion I drove by a backyard laundry line where the two poles supporting the line were painted like green and gold goal posts (and the end zone below contained a pair of errant underpants that had flown in for an apparent touchdown).

But the most impressive sign of a true Packer fan that I witnessed was the painted car syndrome. I think another way of putting it could be, "HOW TO TOTALLY RUIN THE BLUE BOOK VALUE OF YOUR CAR (unless, of course, you sell it to another rabid Packer fanatic, in which case it might increase its value).

Ladies and gentemen, I present to you— THE BRETT VETTE.

A PLATTER FULL OF GOODNESS

The Platter Restaurant

When I first drove up to this interesting old house, I noticed that the parking lot was packed. A good sign, attesting to the popularity and success of a local hot spot.

The locals had highly recommended this place to me. "Great place with a great chef" was the word on the streets of Ashland.

Even though its parking lot was full, I was greeted warmly and soon given a table of my choice, by a window overlooking the Great Lake and its infinite blue water.

I ordered grilled Lake Superior whitefish. It was delicious. The chef and owner, Dave Zeis, came over to my table to talk. He told me about the background of the little restaurant, tucked in among the pines, and about the place that the neighborhood held in history.

A century ago, people vacationed here for their health. It was widely believed that the cool, fresh air rolling off Lake Superior was a natural antidote for hay fever sufferers. People traveled here in droves.

The Lake Superior coastline offered therapeutic rewards for both body and soul. It still does.

"ONCE UPON A TIME, CHILDREN,
THERE WAS ONLY ONE THING ON A STICK . . ."

The Minnesota State Fair

Plain and simple, this is one of the largest state fairs in the country.

Growing up in Minnesota, this was the BIG event of the summer. As a kid growing up in the 1950s, I remember everyone in our neighborhood packing into their station wagons and migrating to the fair grounds in late August, before school started.

Once there, we would head for the rides on the midway, and then stroll the sawdust-covered lanes lined with livestock, candy apple-colored farm machinery, and, of course, the food vendors.

I recall snow cones, cotton candy, mini-donuts, and ONLY ONE THING ON A STICK—the Pronto Pup.

Now, fast-forward a half-century to today's State Fair, and HOLY COW! Everything in the world is on a stick! Over 30 different edible items, all on a stick!

Pronto Pup? Hey, it's there by the ton. But it's a world of inclusion, so everyone is in on this. To mention just a few items, there is Alligator on a Stick, Chicken on a Stick (sounds like a polka song), Scotch Eggs on a Stick, Pork Chop on a Stick, Deep-Fried Pickles on a Stick (Hmmm, deep fried?), Chocolate-Covered

Cheesecake on a Stick, Teriyaki Ostrich!!! on a Stick, and—this is truly for Wisconsin stickoholics:

WALLEYE AND PRIME RIB ON A STICK!!!

Wisconsin eater alert: Could this be heaven?

So, fire up the station wagon (excuse me, the minivan) and head for the fair, folks. Nowadays, it's a great place to practice your stick handling.

(Not to be left out, I'm offering up my own version. I call it SHTICK on a STICK.)

What the Heck?

Nestled deep in a northern boreal forest, this vintage log cabin inn serves up rustic charm and friendliness in lumberjack portions.

Before delving into its history, I need to unearth the answer to the obvious question: THE NAME! How did it acquire the name???

The cabin was originally built in 1935 by the Harper family. For years, it was a well-known steak house, popular among locals and the occasional Chicago gangster who sauntered through its doorway.

Later on, the establishment was named The Capri, and featured the first TV set in the area (which obviously was a big draw). In 1980, Marilyn Heck bought The Capri and decided to change its name. Two friends suggested that she use her own name. Hey, WHAT THE HECK?

So it came to be that this tiny dot on the map has the most Wisconsin-sounding name that I encountered on my journey through the Northland.

But that's not the end of this story. Several years ago, a young couple gave up successful careers in the city to search for their roots. They had grown up on a small town not far away from here. So they bought a lake cabin nearby, packed their bags, and moved up here for good.

Shortly after their move, they bought this little corner side business, rolled up their sleeves, and carried on a rich tradition of good food, good times, and good company. What the Heck? Now THAT sounds good to me.

Eat My Fish

One sunny August day, I found myself driving along a winding road just a few miles shy of Menominee. I was a man on a mission. I was looking for the last fish fry for **Codfather 2.**

A number of people had recommended this "last great place," a little log cafe resting on a corner of the Northland just a few miles ahead.

It was a beautiful day, one of those days when you feel grateful to be alive and traveling in the great outdoors. At the crest of a hill, I zoomed past a little hand-lettered wooden sign that pointed down a narrow, dusty road that meandered over a range of smoky blue hills. The sign read, EAT MY FISH—FOUR MILES.

What? I was a quarter-mile past the sign before I decided, "I can't continue on this trip until I find out what that sign is about."

I will be the first to admit that I have these inner battles with schedules and time. In the past, a little voice within commanded, "DON'T STOP! MAKE TIME! MEET YOUR SCHEDULE!

However, in recent years I've decided to change that pace of life. I've decided to slow down and TAKE TIME to enjoy the journey. So I turned around, went down the dusty road, and took the risk that this could be a four-mile dead-end experience.

The road twisted down into a lush emerald-green valley. In the center of the valley was a collection of jade-green ponds. And near the largest pond was wood frame building. A small hand-lettered sign read, EAT MY FISH—BULLFROG FISH FARM.

So it came to pass that, on this sunny late summer afternoon, I was introduced to my first fish farm. A place where one can step over to the shoreline of one of the ponds and fish for rainbow trout. BIG RAINBOW TROUT. Or, for the less adventurous, buy a fresh trout at the little shop on the grounds. Either option is reasonably priced and includes the intrinsic qualities of unstructured and unhurried time spent in God's Country.

For me, the experience had an added reward.

The lesson learned: It pays to follow your instincts, to take time to explore and seek the answer to what lies on the far side of distant hills.

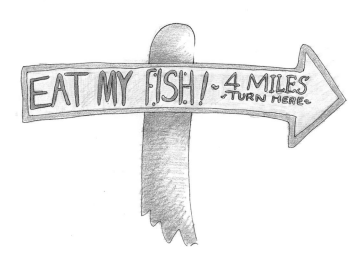

THOUGHTS FROM A SMALL CABIN IN THE FAR NORTH

Bungalow #4

So, here I am at the end of a long and interesting journey. I've pulled off the road and rented a small cabin, Cabin Number 4, to be exact. One of those charming little Ma-and-Pa resorts from the 1940s.

I wanted to reflect on the pages of this book and on the great places and people that I met along its route. But first, I want to describe this little cozy roadside edifice. It's just big enough for a bed, a shower, a kitchen, a vintage TV set that picks up three stations in fuzzy gray images, and a 1950s chrome and green Formica table, just large enough for my sketchbook, my laptop, and a thick mug of Northwoods coffee. For me, it's perfect.

It's a little place, plain and simple. Kind of like this book.

But it's one of the discoveries I made on this journey and in the writing about it. I ventured out to more than 150 places in the upper Midwest that serve fish in one form or another. Big and small, architecturally relevant and neo-nothing. Both famous and not so famous. Big city and little crossroad towns alike. I chose 30 of those for **Codfather 2**. Not for what the "official food critics" said about them, but for what people said about them. For this is a common man's book, a common man's journey.

To echo one of the pages in this book, I found a common thread that connects all of them. It is something that does not appear on the menu or in magazine reviews of these establishments. It is better than that. Better than mere words.

It is a spirit. It is a soul. I stumbled across it one night when I realized that all I needed to do was to slow down the speed of life and look around. Look and enjoy the little places out there on the roadmap of life. It can be found there in the geography of humanity. This may surprise you, but IT AIN'T THE FISH. It's the people, and the friendly atmosphere, that prevail.

It's simple. It's pure. It's the realization that, in the smallest of places, can be found the greatest of rewards.

Small places with big hearts. May your journey in life be as enlightening and rewarding.

JEFF MADEN CABIN #4.

Where to Find Fish

The Port Hotel
101 East Main St.
Port Washington, WI 53074
262 284-9473 or
262 377-6195

Tavern on Grand
656 Grand Ave.
St. Paul, MN 55105
651 228-9030

Trail Center Lodge
7611 Gunflint Trail
Grand Marais, MN 55604
218 388-2214
trailctr@boreal.org

The Longbranch Restaurant
On State Street in
Downtown L'erable
Clifton, IL 60927
815 694-9748

Breitbach's Bar
& Restaurant
563 Balltown Road
Balltown, IA 52073
319 552-2220

Brewery Creek
Brewing Company
23 Commerce St.
Mineral Point, WI 53565
608 987-3298

The Post House
127 East Jefferson
Spring Green, WI 53588
608 588-2595

Partridge Hall
200 S. State St.
Argyle, WI 53504
608 543-3960

Cayuga Hotel Saloon
Route 1, Box 139
Mellen, WI 54546
715 274-5399

Fireman's Tavern
158 E. James St.
Columbus, WI 53925
920 623-3879

Kropp's Supper Club
4570 Shawano Ave.
Green Bay, WI 54313
920 865-7331

Tomorrow River
Supper Club
9971 Highway 10
Amherst, WI 54406
715 824-3113

The Idlewile Inn
1306 Main St.
St. Cloud, WI 53079
920 999-4404

Lelle's Bar
10740 Main St.
Woodford, WI 53599
608 465-3300

What the Heck? Tavern
Corner of County
Hwys A & E
Spooner, WI 54801
715 635-7500

Miss Katie's Diner
1900 W. Clybourn St.
Milwaukee, WI 53233
414 344-0044

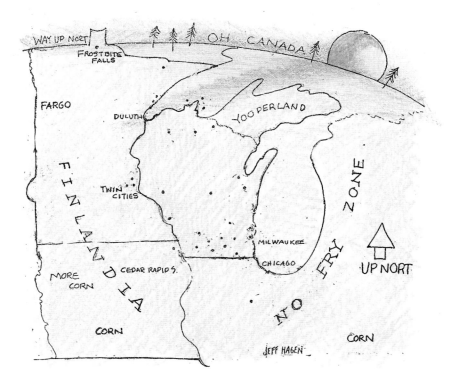

Lake Superior
Big Top Chautauqua
P.O. Box 455
Washburn, WI 54891
715 779-3227
(fish boil information)
715 373-5552
(information on events)

Herbster Town Smelt Fry
Annually, third Saturday
in April
Log gym, one block
south of Hwy. 13
in the center of town

Minnesota State Fair
Annually, the 12 days
before Labor Day
Minnesota State Fair
Grounds, St. Paul

Hubbard Avenue Diner
7445 Hubbard Ave.
Middleton, WI 53562
608 831-6800

Russ Kendall's
Smokehouse
Box 149, Old Hwy. 61
(southern edge of town)
Knife River, MN 55609
218 834-5995

Emily's Deli
Box 174, Old Hwy. 61,
northern edge of town
Knife River, MN 55609
218 834-5922

Eat My Fish /
Bullfrog Fish Farm
N1321 Bullfrog Rd. (12 miles
south of town)
Menominee, WI 54751
715 664-8775
www.eatmyfish.com

Trailways Inn
16021 W. County Rd. K
Hayward, WI 54843
715 634-2328

Fitzgerald's Genoa Junction
727 Main St.
Genoa City, WI 53128
262 279-5200

Easy Creek Bistro
N 6210 County Rd. N
Arkansaw, WI 54721
715 285-5736

Crocus Restaurant
3577 S. 13th St.
Milwaukee, WI 53215
414 643-6383

Greunke's First Street Inn
P.O. Box 768
17 Rittenhouse Ave.
Bayfield, WI 54814
715 779-5480
Toll-free 800 245-3072

Zeis's Platter Restaurant
315 Turner Rd.
Ashland, WI 54806
715 682-2626

The Dining Room
at 209 Main Street
209 Main St.
Monticello, WI 53570
608 938-2200

Gluek's Restaurant
16 N. Sixth St.
Minneapolis, MN 55403

Club 26
N898 Hwy. 26
Fort Atkinson, WI 53538
920 563-9301

Sky Lawn Supper Club
Rt. 1, Box 444
(on Hwy 51, south
of Hurley)
Hurley, WI 54534
715 561-3545

FISH ⚬ FRY

Family Style

ST. PETER'S PARISH - ASHTON

DATE: Oct. 23

PLACE: SCHOOL HALL

SERVING TIME: 4:30 - 8:30

CARRY OUTS AVAILABLE

HOME COOKING COUNTRY STYLE

Hope To See You!

About the Author

Jeff Hagen is a best-selling author and artist of six published books, including two award winners: **Steeple Chase** and **Hiawatha Passing**. The latter was acclaimed by numerous critics, including the Milwaukee Journal, Publishers Weekly, Kirkus Reviews, N.E.A., the

The author (on right) in Paris

Junior Library Guild of America, and the New York Times, which honored it as one of the ten best children's books in America (1995).

Jeff also writes and illustrates cover stories and travel features for many regional and national newspapers, including the Chicago Tribune, St. Paul Pioneer Press, Sunday Detroit News, Minneapolis Star and Tribune, Wisconsin State Journal, Capital Times, and Milwaukee Journal Sentinel. His stories and artwork have appeared in Wisconsin Trails, Cricket, and Outside magazines. Internationally, his work has appeared in the Beijing Review in the People's Republic of China.

He is in frequent demand as a guest speaker and storyteller at public schools, libraries, and universities. His paintings and drawings have appeared in juried shows and exhibits across the United States and in Europe.

He is a frequent guest author on the Wisconsin Public Radio Network and his books have been featured on TV's Food Channel and Good Morning America.

FIN!